PRINCEWILL LAGANG

Infinite Horizons: Larry Page and the Evolution of Google

First published by PRINCEWILL LAGANG 2023

Copyright © 2023 by Princewill Lagang

All rights reserved. No part of this publication may be reproduced, stored or transmitted in any form or by any means, electronic, mechanical, photocopying, recording, scanning, or otherwise without written permission from the publisher. It is illegal to copy this book, post it to a website, or distribute it by any other means without permission.

Princewill Lagang asserts the moral right to be identified as the author of this work.

First edition

*This book was professionally typeset on Reedsy.
Find out more at reedsy.com*

Contents

1	The Genesis of a Visionary	1
2	Code and Culture: The Architectural Foundations of Google	4
3	The Google Ecosystem: A World of Platforms and Paradigms	7
4	Nexus of Innovation: Google's Moonshots and Ambitious...	10
5	Data and Dilemmas: Google in the Age of Information	13
6	Google and Beyond: Transformations, Leadership, and Legacy	16
7	Beyond the Horizon: Challenges, Adaptations, and Google's...	19
8	Infinite Horizons Unveiled: Google's Enduring Impact on...	22
9	Reflections on Infinite Horizons: Google's Journey and...	25
10	Infinite Horizons Explored: A Call to Innovation and...	28
11	Infinite Horizons: A Living Narrative	31
12	Reflections on Infinite Horizons: A Conversation with the...	34
13	Summary	37

1

The Genesis of a Visionary

Title: "Infinite Horizons: Larry Page and the Evolution of Google"

The early morning sun cast a warm glow over the Stanford University campus as Larry Page ambled across the manicured lawns. It was a seemingly ordinary day in the fall of 1995, but little did he know that his casual stroll would mark the inception of a technological revolution. As a Ph.D. student in computer science, Page was steeped in the world of algorithms and data, but on this particular day, a seed of an idea was planted that would transform the digital landscape forever.

1.1 The Spark of Innovation

Larry Page, a brilliant and inquisitive mind, found inspiration in the labyrinthine halls of Stanford. It was here that he began to ponder a fundamental question: How could the vast expanse of the World Wide Web be organized and navigated more efficiently? The internet, burgeoning with information, lacked a coherent structure, and Page was determined to change that.

1.2 The Birth of a Search Engine

As Page delved into his research, he teamed up with Sergey Brin, a fellow Ph.D. student who shared his passion for unraveling the complexities of the web. Together, they embarked on a journey to create a search engine that would not just index pages but understand the context and relevance of information. The duo's collaboration laid the groundwork for what would soon become Google.

1.3 Backrub to Google: The Naming Saga

The name 'Google' didn't materialize overnight. Initially named 'Backrub,' the search engine underwent a series of transformations before Larry Page and Sergey Brin settled on the quirky portmanteau 'Google'—a play on the word 'googol,' reflecting the vastness of information they aimed to organize.

1.4 A Dorm Room Revolution

In the confines of a nondescript dorm room at Stanford, Page and Brin set up the first Google server. Little did they know that this modest server would evolve into a global infrastructure, processing billions of search queries every day. The dorm room, now legendary in Silicon Valley lore, became the birthplace of one of the most influential companies in the world.

1.5 The Stanford Connection

Stanford University, a crucible of innovation, played a pivotal role in shaping the destinies of Larry Page and Sergey Brin. The academic freedom and collaborative spirit at Stanford provided the fertile ground for their revolutionary ideas to take root. The university's ethos of pushing boundaries and challenging the status quo became an integral part of Google's DNA.

1.6 From Research Project to Corporate Giant

As the search engine gained traction, Page and Brin recognized the need to turn their academic project into a viable business. In 1998, Google was officially incorporated, marking the beginning of its ascent from a research endeavor to a corporate giant. The world was about to witness the unfolding of infinite horizons.

In the subsequent chapters, we will explore the challenges, triumphs, and paradigm-shifting moments that defined Google's evolution. From the company's humble beginnings to its role in shaping the digital era, "Infinite Horizons" will trace the fascinating journey of Larry Page and Google, a journey that continues to redefine the way we access and interact with information on the vast canvas of the internet.

2

Code and Culture: The Architectural Foundations of Google

The clatter of keyboards and the hum of servers filled the air as Google's headquarters took shape in the heart of Silicon Valley. Larry Page and Sergey Brin, now at the helm of their burgeoning company, were not just building a search engine; they were constructing a cultural and technological powerhouse. Chapter 2 of "Infinite Horizons" delves into the intricate web of code and culture that became the backbone of Google.

2.1 Engineering Excellence

At the core of Google's success lies a commitment to engineering excellence. The company attracted some of the brightest minds in computer science, creating a culture where innovation and problem-solving were not just encouraged but celebrated. The engineering ethos, instilled by Page and Brin, became synonymous with Google's identity.

2.2 PageRank: The Algorithmic Breakthrough

Central to Google's search algorithm was PageRank, a groundbreaking innovation that went beyond keyword matching. Page and Brin's brainchild, PageRank, analyzed the link structure of the web, considering not only the content of pages but also the connections between them. This revolutionary approach transformed Google's search results into a sophisticated ranking system, setting it apart from competitors.

2.3 Scalability and Infrastructure

As user traffic surged, the need for a robust infrastructure became paramount. Google's engineers faced the challenge of designing systems that could handle the ever-expanding volume of data. The development of the Google File System (GFS) and MapReduce, among other technologies, paved the way for the creation of an infrastructure that could scale seamlessly to meet the demands of a growing digital landscape.

2.4 Cultural Quirks: The Googleplex

Beyond the lines of code, Google nurtured a distinctive corporate culture. The Googleplex, the company's headquarters, embodied a playful and collaborative environment. From colorful bicycles for employees to traverse the sprawling campus to the whimsical design of workspaces, Google's culture fostered creativity and camaraderie.

2.5 "Don't Be Evil": The Ethical Imperative

An unofficial motto but deeply ingrained in Google's philosophy was the phrase "Don't Be Evil." This ethical imperative reflected the company's commitment to responsible and transparent practices. However, as Google expanded its reach and influence, questions arose about the practical implications of this lofty principle.

2.6 Diversification and Innovation

As Google solidified its dominance in search, Page and Brin were not content to rest on their laurels. The company diversified its portfolio, venturing into email with Gmail, mapping with Google Maps, and, perhaps most notably, acquiring YouTube. These strategic moves demonstrated Google's commitment to innovation and its ambition to shape not only how information was found but also how it was shared and consumed.

Chapter 2 unveils the intricate dance between technology and culture that defined Google's formative years. From algorithmic breakthroughs to quirky corporate campuses, the chapter sets the stage for the next phase of Google's evolution—one marked by both unprecedented success and the challenges of maintaining a delicate balance between innovation and ethical responsibility.

3

The Google Ecosystem: A World of Platforms and Paradigms

As the new millennium dawned, Google was no longer just a search engine; it had become an expansive ecosystem, shaping the digital landscape in ways that reverberated across industries. Chapter 3 of "Infinite Horizons" explores the evolution of Google's ecosystem— a complex interplay of products, platforms, and paradigms that transformed the company into a technological behemoth.

3.1 Google's Acquisition Spree

The early 2000s witnessed a strategic acquisition spree by Google, as the company sought to expand its capabilities and influence. From the acquisition of Android in 2005, which laid the foundation for Google's mobile dominance, to the purchase of Keyhole, a mapping technology that would evolve into Google Earth, each acquisition was a puzzle piece in the construction of a multifaceted digital empire.

3.2 Mobile Revolution: Android and Beyond

The launch of the Android operating system marked Google's foray into the mobile realm. Initially envisioned as an open-source platform for smartphones, Android soon became the dominant force in the mobile ecosystem. Google's presence extended beyond search to include applications like Google Maps, Gmail, and the Play Store, transforming mobile devices into indispensable tools for users around the globe.

3.3 Cloud Computing: Google's Ascent to the Clouds

Recognizing the shift towards cloud computing, Google invested heavily in cloud infrastructure and services. The introduction of Google Cloud Platform (GCP) positioned the company as a key player in the cloud computing market, competing with industry giants. The cloud became not only a technological backbone for businesses but also a strategic frontier for Google's expansion.

3.4 Social Networking and the Rise of Google+

In an attempt to challenge the dominance of Facebook, Google launched its own social networking platform, Google+. While it ultimately fell short of becoming a Facebook competitor, Google+ highlighted the company's eagerness to diversify and explore new frontiers, even if met with occasional setbacks.

3.5 Challenges and Controversies

With great success came great scrutiny. Google faced growing concerns about user privacy, antitrust issues, and criticisms of its handling of user data. The company's commitment to "Don't Be Evil" was questioned as it navigated the fine line between innovation and ethical responsibility. The chapter delves into how these challenges shaped Google's approach to corporate responsibility and its relationships with regulators and users.

3.6 The Paradigm Shift: Machine Learning and AI

Embracing the era of artificial intelligence, Google made significant strides in machine learning and AI applications. From the introduction of Google Photos' image recognition to the integration of AI in search algorithms, the company pushed the boundaries of what was possible, ushering in a new era of intelligent computing.

As Chapter 3 unfolds, it reveals a Google that transcends its origins as a search engine. The company's expansion into mobile, cloud, social networking, and artificial intelligence laid the groundwork for a digital ecosystem that touched every aspect of our lives. The chapter not only explores Google's triumphs but also confronts the growing challenges and controversies that accompanied its ascent to digital dominance.

4

Nexus of Innovation: Google's Moonshots and Ambitious Endeavors

In the sprawling landscape of Silicon Valley, where innovation knows no bounds, Google stood as a beacon of audacity. Chapter 4 of "Infinite Horizons" delves into the world of Google's moonshots and ambitious endeavors—projects that stretched the limits of imagination and redefined the very notion of what a tech company could achieve.

4.1 X, Alphabet, and the Moonshot Factory

As Google continued to evolve, Larry Page and Sergey Brin restructured the company in 2015, creating Alphabet Inc. as the parent company overseeing various subsidiaries, each operating as an independent entity. The secretive Google X lab, later renamed X, became the birthplace of moonshots—ambitious projects with the potential to revolutionize industries and solve some of humanity's most pressing challenges.

4.2 Project Loon: Balloons in the Stratosphere

In an effort to bridge the digital divide, Project Loon aimed to provide internet access to remote and underserved regions using high-altitude balloons. The chapter explores the technical challenges, triumphs, and the ultimate decision to retire the project, highlighting Google's willingness to experiment even when faced with formidable obstacles.

4.3 Waymo: Driving into the Future

Autonomous vehicles were not just a moonshot; they were a revolution in transportation. Waymo, a subsidiary of Alphabet, emerged from Google's self-driving car project. The chapter explores the journey from the first autonomous car prototypes to the deployment of Waymo's self-driving taxis on the streets, reshaping the future of transportation.

4.4 Project Wing: Drones for Deliveries

Project Wing sought to revolutionize logistics by using drones for deliveries. The chapter uncovers the challenges of navigating regulatory hurdles and public perceptions, showcasing how Google's moonshots often faced not only technical obstacles but also societal and regulatory challenges.

4.5 Life Sciences: Verily's Pursuit of Health Tech

Under the Alphabet umbrella, Verily Life Sciences aimed to transform healthcare through technology. The chapter explores Verily's ambitious projects, from developing smart contact lenses to advanced health monitoring systems, and the broader implications of technology in the healthcare landscape.

4.6 Moonshots Beyond Alphabet: Google Brain and DeepMind

Beyond Alphabet, Google Brain and DeepMind pushed the boundaries of artificial intelligence. The chapter delves into how these projects advanced machine learning and AI, from the development of neural networks to landmark achievements in gaming and healthcare.

4.7 Beyond Earth: Google's Space Ambitions

Google's fascination with space exploration extended beyond our planet. The chapter explores Google's investments in space ventures, including collaborations with SpaceX and the exploration of satellite technology, showcasing the company's willingness to reach for the stars.

Chapter 4 unfolds as a chronicle of Google's most daring ventures, ventures that epitomize the company's commitment to pushing the boundaries of innovation. From internet-beaming balloons to self-driving cars and beyond, the chapter encapsulates the spirit of exploration that defines Google's moonshots and their potential to shape the future in ways unimaginable.

5

Data and Dilemmas: Google in the Age of Information

As Google expanded its reach and influence, it found itself at the intersection of immense data resources and profound societal impact. Chapter 5 of "Infinite Horizons" delves into the evolving role of Google in the age of information, exploring the opportunities, challenges, and ethical dilemmas that emerged as the company became an integral part of the global digital landscape.

5.1 Data as Currency: Google's Dominance in Advertising

With its powerful search engine and a growing suite of services, Google amassed an unparalleled trove of user data. The chapter unravels how this data became the lifeblood of the company's advertising empire, enabling targeted and personalized advertisements that not only fueled Google's revenue but also transformed the digital advertising landscape.

5.2 The Rise of Google Analytics and User Tracking

Google Analytics emerged as a cornerstone of the digital marketing ecosystem, offering businesses unprecedented insights into user behavior. However, this data-driven era raised concerns about user privacy and surveillance. The chapter explores the balance between data-driven marketing and the ethical implications of extensive user tracking.

5.3 Privacy Paradox: The Double-Edged Sword

As Google endeavored to provide personalized services, the tension between customization and user privacy intensified. The chapter delves into the paradox of privacy, examining Google's efforts to navigate the delicate balance between offering tailored user experiences and safeguarding individuals' privacy rights.

5.4 Search Neutrality and Algorithmic Biases

The chapter sheds light on the concept of search neutrality and the challenges Google faced in maintaining an unbiased search engine. It explores instances of algorithmic biases and the debates surrounding the responsibility of tech companies to ensure fair and impartial access to information.

5.5 Government Scrutiny and Antitrust Investigations

As Google's influence grew, so did scrutiny from regulatory bodies. The chapter examines the antitrust investigations and legal challenges faced by Google, exploring the company's responses to allegations of monopolistic practices and its impact on the broader tech industry.

5.6 Fake News and Disinformation: Google's Role in Information Integrity

Google found itself in the crossfire of the battle against fake news and disinformation. The chapter explores the measures taken by the company to combat misinformation, from refining search algorithms to promoting fact-checking initiatives and the broader implications for the role of tech companies in shaping public discourse.

5.7 The Right to Be Forgotten and Global Internet Governance

The concept of the "Right to Be Forgotten" emerged as a pivotal legal and ethical issue. The chapter examines Google's responses to requests for content removal and the challenges of navigating global internet governance, where cultural, legal, and ethical norms vary widely.

Chapter 5 unfolds as a nuanced exploration of Google's complex relationship with data, privacy, and societal impact. From advertising dominance to the challenges of combating misinformation, the chapter reflects the intricate dance between technological innovation and the ethical dilemmas that arise in an era where information is both a commodity and a potential source of societal disruption.

6

Google and Beyond: Transformations, Leadership, and Legacy

As the digital landscape continued to evolve, so did Google. Chapter 6 of "Infinite Horizons" unfolds as a reflection on the transformations, leadership transitions, and the enduring legacy of a company that forever changed how we interact with information and technology.

6.1 Leadership Evolution: Sundar Pichai's Google

Larry Page and Sergey Brin, the visionary duo behind Google's inception, stepped back from day-to-day leadership roles in 2019, placing Sundar Pichai at the helm of both Google and Alphabet. The chapter explores the leadership transition and Pichai's strategic vision for steering the company through a new era of challenges and opportunities.

6.2 Alphabet's Portfolio: The Evolution of a Conglomerate

Under Alphabet's umbrella, subsidiaries diversified and matured. The chapter delves into how Alphabet's structure allowed for a more focused approach to diverse industries, from healthcare to autonomous vehicles, showcasing the intricate tapestry of innovation that defined the conglomerate's portfolio.

6.3 Google's Cultural Shifts: From "Don't Be Evil" to Responsible AI

The chapter explores Google's cultural shifts over the years, from the informal and entrepreneurial ethos of its early days to a more structured and accountable corporate culture. It examines how the company grappled with maintaining its founding principles, particularly in the context of artificial intelligence and responsible technology development.

6.4 Privacy and User Control: Google's Ongoing Challenges

Privacy concerns persisted, and the chapter examines how Google responded to growing public awareness and regulatory pressures. It explores initiatives to give users more control over their data, including privacy features and tools, and the ongoing dialogue between tech companies, users, and regulators on data protection.

6.5 Continued Innovations: AI, Quantum Computing, and Beyond

Google remained at the forefront of technological innovation. The chapter explores the company's advancements in artificial intelligence, quantum computing, and other emerging fields. It reflects on how these innovations continued to shape the digital landscape and redefine the possibilities of what technology could achieve.

6.6 Global Impact and Social Responsibility

As one of the world's most influential companies, Google faced increasing scrutiny regarding its societal impact. The chapter delves into Google's initiatives in corporate social responsibility, environmental sustainability, and philanthropy, exploring the company's efforts to contribute positively to the communities it served.

6.7 Legacy and Future Vistas: Google in the Next Frontier

The chapter concludes by reflecting on Google's legacy and its future. It examines the lasting impact of the company on technology, information access, and the broader digital ecosystem. It also speculates on the potential directions Google might take as it faces new challenges and opportunities in the ever-evolving landscape of the information age.

Chapter 6 serves as a contemplative look at Google's journey from its humble beginnings in a Stanford dorm room to its status as a global tech giant. It explores the company's ability to adapt, innovate, and grapple with the complexities of leadership, societal impact, and the relentless pursuit of infinite horizons in the digital realm.

7

Beyond the Horizon: Challenges, Adaptations, and Google's Enduring Influence

The final chapter of "Infinite Horizons" delves into the contemporary landscape of Google, examining the challenges faced by the tech giant, its adaptive strategies, and the enduring influence it continues to wield in the ever-evolving digital frontier.

7.1 The Evolving Search Paradigm: From Keywords to Intent

The chapter begins by exploring how Google's search paradigm has evolved. With advancements in natural language processing and machine learning, the focus shifted from keyword matching to understanding user intent. It discusses the implications of this shift on user experience, content creation, and the broader search ecosystem.

7.2 Competition and Market Dynamics

Google's dominance in the search and advertising space has not gone uncontested. The chapter delves into the evolving dynamics of competition, examining the rise of alternative search engines, shifts in advertising landscapes, and the impact of new entrants in the tech industry on Google's market position.

7.3 AI and Ethics: Navigating the Moral Compass

As artificial intelligence becomes increasingly intertwined with everyday technologies, the chapter explores how Google grapples with the ethical dimensions of AI. It examines the company's initiatives to develop AI responsibly, addressing issues of bias, transparency, and the broader societal impacts of AI technologies.

7.4 Regulatory Challenges: Antitrust, Privacy, and Beyond

Google has faced intensified scrutiny from regulators globally. The chapter discusses the ongoing antitrust investigations, privacy regulations, and the company's responses to legal challenges. It explores how regulatory landscapes shape Google's strategies and its implications for the broader tech industry.

7.5 The Mobile-First World: Android, Mobile Apps, and Beyond

The mobile revolution continues to shape how users interact with technology. The chapter explores Google's strategies in the mobile-first world, from the evolution of the Android operating system to the dominance of mobile apps and the challenges and opportunities presented by the mobile ecosystem.

7.6 New Frontiers: Quantum Computing, Augmented Reality, and More

Google continues to explore new frontiers in technology. The chapter examines the company's forays into quantum computing, augmented reality, and other emerging technologies. It reflects on the potential impact of these innovations on industries, societies, and the way we perceive and interact with the digital world.

7.7 Legacy and Future Horizons

The chapter concludes by revisiting Google's legacy and pondering its future horizons. It reflects on the enduring impact of the company on the digital landscape, its contributions to innovation, and the challenges it faces as it navigates an era of rapid technological advancement, societal change, and increasing global interconnectedness.

Chapter 7 encapsulates the contemporary landscape of Google, acknowledging the challenges it faces while highlighting its resilience, adaptability, and ongoing influence in shaping the trajectory of technology and information in the digital age. It serves as both a reflection on Google's journey thus far and a contemplation of the infinite horizons that lie ahead.

8

Infinite Horizons Unveiled: Google's Enduring Impact on Society

The concluding chapter of "Infinite Horizons" transcends the immediate technological landscape to reflect on Google's profound and lasting impact on society. Chapter 8 explores the multifaceted ways in which Google has shaped the world, influencing not only how we access information but also our culture, economy, and the very fabric of our interconnected lives.

8.1 Information Access and Democratization

Google's mission to organize the world's information and make it universally accessible has democratized access to knowledge. The chapter examines how Google has empowered individuals, providing them with unprecedented access to information, breaking down barriers to education, and fostering a more informed and connected global society.

8.2 Economic Transformations: Digital Economy and Entrepreneurship

The advent of Google has catalyzed significant economic transformations.

The chapter explores the rise of the digital economy, the ecosystem of online businesses, and the role of Google in empowering entrepreneurs through platforms like Google Ads, Play Store, and cloud services.

8.3 Cultural Influence: Google as a Cultural Archivist

Google has become a cultural archivist, capturing the zeitgeist of the internet age. The chapter delves into how Google, through search trends, Google Doodles, and initiatives like Google Arts & Culture, has influenced and reflected the cultural fabric of societies around the world.

8.4 Global Connectivity and Collaboration

The chapter explores how Google has contributed to global connectivity and collaboration. Through products like Google Translate and initiatives like Google for Education, the company has facilitated cross-cultural communication, breaking down language barriers and fostering collaboration on a global scale.

8.5 The Rise of Social Impact: Google.org and Beyond

Google's commitment to social impact is examined in this section. The chapter delves into the initiatives led by Google.org, the company's philanthropic arm, and explores how Google's technology has been leveraged for humanitarian efforts, crisis response, and addressing global challenges.

8.6 Challenges of Digital Inclusion and Privacy

While Google has contributed to digital inclusion, the chapter acknowledges the challenges of ensuring equitable access to technology and addressing concerns about privacy. It reflects on the ongoing dialogue between technology companies, policymakers, and society in balancing the benefits of innovation with the need to protect individual rights.

8.7 Educational Influence: Google in Learning and Development

Google has left an indelible mark on education. The chapter explores the impact of Google's suite of educational tools, from Google Classroom to G Suite for Education, and reflects on the company's role in shaping the future of learning and development.

8.8 Beyond Google: The Next Epoch of Innovation

The chapter concludes by contemplating the next epoch of innovation beyond Google. It considers the evolving landscape of technology, emerging trends, and the potential role of new players and disruptors in shaping the digital future.

Chapter 8 serves as a panoramic view of Google's societal impact, acknowledging its transformative influence on information access, economics, culture, global connectivity, and social responsibility. As the company's legacy continues to unfold, the chapter ponders the infinite horizons that extend beyond Google, influencing the trajectory of technology and society for generations to come.

9

Reflections on Infinite Horizons: Google's Journey and Future Trajectories

In the final chapter of "Infinite Horizons," we take a reflective journey through Google's remarkable evolution, exploring key milestones, the company's cultural legacy, and contemplating the potential trajectories that lie ahead in the dynamic landscape of technology and information.

9.1 Milestones Revisited: Pivotal Moments in Google's Odyssey

This section revisits pivotal moments in Google's journey, from its founding in a Stanford dorm room to the introduction of groundbreaking technologies, strategic acquisitions, leadership transitions, and the myriad innovations that have defined the company's trajectory.

9.2 Cultural Legacy: The Google Ethos and Its Enduring Impact

The chapter reflects on the cultural legacy of Google, exploring how the company's ethos of innovation, collaboration, and a commitment to making information universally accessible has left an indelible mark on Silicon Valley and beyond. It examines how elements of the "Google culture" have influenced workplace dynamics, entrepreneurial endeavors, and the broader tech industry.

9.3 Lessons Learned: Challenges, Adaptations, and Corporate Resilience

Examining the challenges Google faced, the chapter extracts valuable lessons from the company's journey. It reflects on how Google navigated regulatory scrutiny, privacy concerns, and the ever-shifting technological landscape, showcasing the adaptive strategies and resilience that contributed to its enduring success.

9.4 Ethical Considerations: Google's Impact on Society and Responsibility

As Google's influence expanded, so did ethical considerations. This section reflects on the ethical implications of Google's actions, decisions, and influence on society. It explores the responsibilities of tech companies in shaping the digital future and the ongoing dialogue around issues such as privacy, data ethics, and the societal impact of technology.

9.5 The Next Chapter: Potential Trajectories and Emerging Trends

The chapter contemplates potential trajectories for Google in the coming years. It explores emerging trends in technology, artificial intelligence, augmented reality, and other fields that may shape the company's future. It also considers the role Google might play in addressing societal challenges, fostering innovation, and contributing to the broader global community.

9.6 Voices from the Future: Perspectives on Google's Impact

This section incorporates perspectives from thought leaders, industry experts, and futurists, offering diverse insights on Google's impact and potential future contributions. It explores how different voices envision the role of Google in an evolving digital landscape and the implications for technology, society, and individual lives.

9.7 Closing the Chapter: Infinite Horizons and Ever-Expanding Frontiers

As the book concludes, it reflects on the concept of "infinite horizons" and the ever-expanding frontiers that define Google's journey. It encapsulates the essence of the company's role in shaping the information age and its potential to continue pushing boundaries in the pursuit of innovation, knowledge, and positive societal impact.

Chapter 9 serves as a reflective coda to "Infinite Horizons," capturing the essence of Google's journey, its cultural legacy, and the possibilities that unfold as the company navigates the next chapters in the unfolding story of technology and humanity.

10

Infinite Horizons Explored: A Call to Innovation and Responsibility

As we draw the final curtain on "Infinite Horizons," Chapter 10 serves as both a summation and a call to action. It explores the continuous journey of innovation, responsibility, and the profound impact of technology on our world. This chapter encourages a forward-looking perspective, challenging both Google and the broader tech industry to navigate the complexities of the digital frontier responsibly.

10.1 The Dynamic Nature of Innovation

This section celebrates the dynamic nature of innovation that has defined Google's trajectory. It reflects on the ever-evolving landscape of technology, emphasizing the importance of adaptability, creativity, and a relentless pursuit of knowledge as key drivers of progress.

10.2 Embracing Responsible Technology

Building on Google's mantra of "Don't Be Evil," the chapter emphasizes the need for responsible technology. It explores how tech companies, Google included, can proactively address ethical considerations, data privacy, and societal impact, fostering a culture of responsibility that transcends profit margins.

10.3 Empowering Inclusivity and Accessibility

In a world where technology can be a powerful force for inclusivity, this section examines the role of Google and other tech leaders in ensuring that innovation is inclusive. It delves into efforts to bridge digital divides, provide access to information for all, and amplify diverse voices in the tech ecosystem.

10.4 Environmental Stewardship and Sustainability

With an increasing focus on environmental sustainability, the chapter explores Google's role in environmental stewardship. It delves into initiatives to reduce carbon footprints, invest in renewable energy, and promote sustainable practices within the tech industry.

10.5 Education as a Catalyst for Change

Education emerges as a catalyst for societal transformation. The chapter explores the role of technology, especially educational tools and platforms, in shaping the minds of future innovators and leaders. It reflects on how Google and similar entities can contribute to educational equity and prepare the next generation for the challenges and opportunities of the digital age.

10.6 Global Collaboration for Positive Impact

Highlighting the interconnectedness of the modern world, this section calls for global collaboration. It explores how tech companies can work collaboratively with governments, non-profits, and other stakeholders to address global challenges, leveraging technology for positive societal impact.

10.7 The Enduring Spirit of Innovation

As the book concludes, it underscores the enduring spirit of innovation that propels humanity forward. It encourages Google and other tech pioneers to continue pushing boundaries, exploring uncharted territories, and embracing the responsibility that comes with shaping the future of our interconnected world.

10.8 A Continued Conversation: Engaging with the Infinite Horizons

This final section invites readers, industry professionals, and thought leaders to engage in a continued conversation. It encourages ongoing dialogue about the evolving role of technology in society, the responsibilities of tech companies, and the infinite horizons that await exploration.

Chapter 10 serves as a rallying cry for innovation tempered with responsibility. It challenges not only Google but also all stakeholders in the technological landscape to embrace a shared vision of a future where the infinite horizons of innovation are navigated with a deep sense of ethical responsibility, inclusivity, and a commitment to positive global impact.

11

Infinite Horizons: A Living Narrative

In a departure from conventional conclusions, Chapter 11 serves as an open-ended exploration, acknowledging that the story of Google and the broader technological narrative is far from over. It considers the dynamic nature of innovation, societal evolution, and the unpredictable twists that may shape the future.

11.1 The Unfinished Story: Technology's Unpredictable Trajectory

This section embraces the idea that the story of technology is an ongoing, dynamic narrative. It reflects on the unforeseen developments, paradigm shifts, and disruptive innovations that may unfold in the years to come. The narrative is open-ended, leaving room for the unexpected.

11.2 Emerging Technologies and Potential Disruptions

The chapter explores emerging technologies that may disrupt the current technological landscape. From advancements in artificial intelligence to breakthroughs in quantum computing and beyond, it speculates on the potential game-changers that could redefine how we interact with information and technology.

11.3 Evolution of Human-Machine Interaction

As technology becomes increasingly intertwined with our daily lives, this section considers the evolution of human-machine interaction. It reflects on the potential for augmented reality, brain-computer interfaces, and other innovations to reshape the way we perceive and engage with the digital world.

11.4 Societal Expectations and Ethical Considerations

Recognizing the pivotal role that societal expectations and ethical considerations play in technology's trajectory, the chapter contemplates how public sentiment, regulatory frameworks, and evolving ethical standards may influence the path of technological innovation.

11.5 The Shifting Sands of Industry Dynamics

Industries are continually transformed by technology. This section considers the potential evolution of industry dynamics, from the rise of new players to shifts in business models and the impact of global events on the tech landscape.

11.6 Global Collaborations and Technological Diplomacy

As technology transcends borders, this part explores the potential for global collaborations and technological diplomacy. It contemplates how nations, corporations, and organizations might work together to address global challenges and harness the power of technology for collective well-being.

11.7 The Role of the Individual: Empowerment and Responsibility

The narrative turns to the individual, emphasizing the role of each person in shaping the technological future. It explores how empowered individuals, equipped with technology, can contribute to positive societal change and ethical innovation.

11.8 Continued Conversations: Engaging with the Living Narrative

This concluding section extends an invitation for continued conversations. It encourages readers, innovators, and thought leaders to actively participate in shaping the ongoing narrative of technology, engaging in discussions, and contributing to the collective wisdom that guides the evolution of our digital future.

Chapter 11 stands as an acknowledgment of the perpetual nature of innovation and invites readers to become co-authors in the unfolding narrative of technology. It sparks curiosity, embraces uncertainty, and celebrates the infinite horizons that await exploration in the ever-changing landscape of the digital age.

12

Reflections on Infinite Horizons: A Conversation with the Future

As we approach the final chapter of "Infinite Horizons," we engage in a unique format—an imagined conversation with the future. This chapter is a dialogue that explores the impact of the technological journey chronicled in the book and speculates on the potential trajectories that lie ahead.

12.1 Looking Back: Google's Impact on Society

In this part of the conversation, we reflect on the impact of Google's journey. We explore how the innovations, cultural shifts, and societal changes influenced by Google have shaped the way people live, work, and interact with information. The dialogue delves into the lasting impressions left on education, culture, and global connectivity.

12.2 Challenges Overcome and Lessons Learned

The imagined conversation delves into the challenges Google faced and overcame throughout its evolution. It explores the lessons learned, adaptive strategies employed, and how these experiences contributed to the resilience and ongoing success of the company.

12.3 Ethical Considerations: From "Don't Be Evil" to Responsible Innovation

In this segment, the dialogue delves into the ethical considerations that emerged along the way. It reflects on how Google and the broader tech industry navigated these challenges, moved beyond the unofficial motto "Don't Be Evil," and embraced a culture of responsible innovation.

12.4 Emerging Technologies: A Glimpse into the Future

The conversation shifts to the future, speculating on emerging technologies that may redefine the technological landscape. It explores the potential impact of advancements in artificial intelligence, quantum computing, biotechnology, and other fields, offering a glimpse into the transformative possibilities ahead.

12.5 The Role of Society: Empowerment and Responsibility

Acknowledging the symbiotic relationship between technology and society, the dialogue examines the evolving role of individuals and communities. It considers how empowered individuals, informed by lessons from the past, can actively shape the trajectory of technology, emphasizing the importance of responsible engagement and ethical considerations.

12.6 Environmental Sustainability and Global Collaboration

Addressing the growing importance of environmental sustainability, the conversation explores how technology can be harnessed to address global challenges. It contemplates collaborative efforts on a global scale, bringing together nations, corporations, and individuals to work towards a sustainable and equitable future.

12.7 Educational Transformations: Nurturing the Innovators of Tomorrow

The dialogue turns to the realm of education, considering how technological innovations have transformed learning. It explores the role of technology in nurturing the innovators of tomorrow, fostering a culture of curiosity, critical thinking, and adaptability.

12.8 Continued Narratives: Inviting Ongoing Conversations

As the imagined conversation concludes, it extends an invitation for ongoing dialogue. It emphasizes the importance of continued conversations, reflections, and active engagement with the ever-unfolding narrative of technology, encouraging readers and stakeholders to play an integral role in shaping the future.

Chapter 12 serves as a contemplative and speculative conclusion—a conversation with the future that invites readers to consider the impact of technological evolution, reflect on the lessons learned, and actively participate in the ongoing narrative of innovation and responsibility.

13

Summary

"Infinite Horizons" is a comprehensive exploration of Google's journey from its inception in a Stanford dorm room to its status as a global technology giant. The book unfolds through twelve chapters, each delving into different facets of Google's evolution, impact on society, and the challenges it faced. From Larry Page and Sergey Brin's early vision to the emergence of Google as a multifaceted ecosystem, the narrative traverses key milestones, moonshot projects, ethical considerations, and the company's enduring influence.

Chapters 1 to 6 provide an in-depth look at Google's foundational years, its expansion into various technological frontiers, and the development of moonshot projects that pushed the boundaries of innovation. Chapter 7 explores the contemporary landscape, addressing challenges, adaptations, and Google's continued influence. Chapters 8 and 9 delve into Google's societal impact, reflecting on its contributions to information access, economic transformation, cultural influence, and social responsibility.

Chapters 10 and 11 serve as calls to action, urging the tech industry to embrace responsible innovation, inclusivity, and environmental sustainability. Chapter 12 takes a unique approach, presenting an imagined conversation with the future, reflecting on Google's impact, lessons learned, and speculating on emerging technologies and societal roles.

The book is not just a historical account but a forward-looking exploration, inviting readers to engage in ongoing conversations about the ever-evolving narrative of technology. It emphasizes the dynamic nature of innovation, ethical considerations, and the role of individuals and society in shaping the future. "Infinite Horizons" serves as both a chronicle of Google's journey and a contemplative guide for navigating the uncharted territories of the digital age.

www.ingramcontent.com/pod-product-compliance
Lightning Source LLC
LaVergne TN
LVHW020456080526
838202LV00057B/5976